Rejected,
Yet
Loved

To
is Robin
my long time
friend.
Be inspired as you
read this book. Thanks
for your support, prayers
& love.
Be blessed!
Love you
Laurie
10/1/10

Rejected,
Yet
Loved

Leah – The Rejected One

Lauri V. Mack

Aventine Press

Unless otherwise noted, all scripture quotations are from the King James Version of the Bible.

Printed in the United States of America

Cover design by Desere` Mayo

isbn: 1-59330-678-4

TABLE OF CONTENTS

DEDICATION

This book is in memory of my loving husband, Bruce Mack. You were my best friend, my lover and my supporter, and I love you with all of my heart!

To my birth children: Gregory Montel McNeal and Desere` Dionna Mayo whom I love so very much. Thank you for loving your Mommy through it all!

To my new additions: Bruce Jr., Shammar, Lily, Larry (L), Trena, Brandon and Erica… I love you too!

To women everywhere who at one time was in this situation and God brought you out!

SPECIAL THANKS

I thank my Heavenly Father for the opportunity to minister to women everywhere.

I thank my Pastor, Apostle Toni Pugh, my first lady, Prophetess Alva Pugh, and my brothers and sisters in the Lord with whom I worship with every Sunday morning at Deeper Life Full Gospel Ministries. Thank you for the encouragement and prayers. We really are impacting this world with His Word!!

I especially want to thank Melissa Brown, Linda McKenzie and Brenda Brown for being my editors. I couldn't have completed this without the three of you.

A special thanks goes to Evangelist Yvonne Mallory who inspired me to dig deep and pull out the creativity within.

Thanks also go to Rev. Max Millender who encouraged me to get this book done so that it can be a blessing to the body of Christ. It's your turn now.

A LETTER FROM THE AUTHOR

Dear Reader,

Thank you so much for taking the time to read this book.

Rejected Yet Loved is for the happily married, the one whose marriage is shaky, those who have never been married, and the one who was once married.

My prayer is that this book will bless you and cause you to realize that you are special to God. You are a valuable and essential part of the body of Christ.

You are to be conformed into the image of Christ. Do not allow bitterness to reign in your heart because of what you have gone through, but use the hours of loneliness, the frustration, the waiting game, the pain and rejection as stepping stones in fulfilling your God ordained purpose. Use them to draw nigh to your Heavenly Father because He is drawing nigh to you.

I chose to share some of my experiences before I got married in this book. If I would have dwelled in the hurt and wallowed in the rejection, it would have driven me to depression and perhaps even suicide. I had to keep my focus on Jesus and realize that He loved me no matter what. It was hard sometimes, but I got through it and you will too!

Be blessed as you read this book and I challenge you to let God mend the broken pieces in your life so that you may realize you are loved!

In due season, you shall reap if you faint not.

Love,

Lauri

CHAPTER ONE

LEAH – A CASE OF REJECTION

"And Laban had two daughters; the name of the elder was Leah, and the name of the younger was Rachel. Leah was tender eyed; but Rachel was beautiful and well favored. And Jacob loved Rachel; and said, 'I will serve thee seven years for Rachel thy younger daughter.' And Laban said, 'It is better that I give her to thee, than that I should give her to another man; abide with me.' And Jacob served seven years for Rachel; and they seemed unto him but a few days, for the love he had to her. And Jacob said unto Laban; 'Give me my wife, for my days are fulfilled, that I may go in unto her.' And Laban gathered together all the men of the place, and made a feast. And it came to pass in the evening that he took Leah his daughter, and brought her to him; and he went in unto her. And Laban gave unto his daughter Leah Zilpah his maid for an handmaid. And it came to pass, that in the morning, behold, it was Leah; and he said to Laban, 'What is this thou hast done unto me? Did not I serve with thee for Rachel? Wherefore then hast thou beguiled me?'

*And Laban said, 'It must not be so done in our country, to give the younger before the firstborn. Fulfill her week, and we will give thee this also for the service which thou shalt serve with me yet seven other years.' And Jacob did so, and fulfilled her week: and he gave him Rachel his daughter to wife also. And Laban gave to Rachel his daughter Bilhah his handmaid to be her maid. And he went in also unto Rachel, and he loved also Rachel more than Leah, and served with him yet seven other years. And when **the Lord saw that Leah was hated, he opened her womb**: but Rachel was barren. And Leah conceived, and bare a son, and she called his **name Reuben: for she said, 'Surely the Lord hath looked upon my affliction; now therefore my husband will love me.**' And she conceived again, and bare a son; and said, **'Because the Lord hath heard that I was hated, he hath therefore given me this son also:' and she called his name Simeon.** And she conceived again, and bare a son; and said, **'Now this time will my husband be joined unto me, because I have born him three sons;' therefore was his named called Levi.** And she conceived again, and bare a son: and she said, **'Now will I praise the Lord:' therefore she called his name Judah and left bearing."** Genesis 29:16-35.*

From the above scripture, we can see that Leah was the oldest daughter of a man named Laban, who was Jacob's uncle. She was tender eyed, rejected and hated. She became the wife of Jacob which was not by his choice. Leah was married, but did her husband really love her?

Can you imagine marrying a man who is not in love with you and who made love to you on your wedding night thinking that you were someone else? We see that Jacob was highly upset because he said to Laban, "What is this thou hast done unto me?" But how do you think Leah felt? Laban then told Jacob that there was a custom concerning marrying off the oldest daughter first. If that were so, why didn't he tell Jacob at the beginning?

How can a father do something like this to his little girl? There is just something about a father and daughter relationship that is so precious and priceless. With this in mind, I wonder what kind of relationship Laban had with his daughter Leah.

On the night of the marriage, I can imagine that Jacob really had himself a wonderful time with his bride. It was their wedding night and he knew that the marriage bed was undefiled, so it was honeymoon bliss. He loved Rachel so much and now his dream had become a reality. He did not realize that it was not Rachel until the next morning. He had been tricked; but what about Leah?

Your wedding night should be something special, something that you have been waiting for your entire life. You are marrying someone who loves you, a man that makes you feel good, a man who you love, and a man who gets you excited when you are going to be together. He proposes, you say yes, and that special night is going to be a night that you will never forget. That was not the case for Leah.

Here Leah was being made love to by a man that thought she was her sister. She did not say, "Jacob it is not Rachel, its Leah." She did not stop him from making love to her; she accepted what was happening. What kind of thoughts had to be running through her mind, knowing that Jacob loved her sister and not her? What was she thinking when he was kissing her, touching her, and making passionate love to her? After it was over and as she was lying in bed with him, did she go to sleep? How could she, when the man that was making love to her did not know that it was her? Maybe she thought that since he made love to her, he could love her.

Remember Jacob worked for Laban, Leah and Rachel's father for seven years before he married Leah. During that time Leah could have fallen in love with him. Possibly this is the reason she didn't say anything to him when he was making love to her. Keep in mind that the Bible does not tell us this, this is just a thought.

The name Leah means weary. Leah could have been tired of the life that she lived with her father and his servants. She could have wanted a different, and what she may have thought to be, a better life. She needed a change.

Being the oldest daughter you have added responsibilities. You are in charge of making sure that the rest of your siblings' chores are done. You are responsible for your siblings if your parents are away. The oldest daughter is the one, who is in the kitchen with mom learning how to cook. While the rest of your siblings are outside playing, you have work to do. This is how it is in a lot of homes even today; the oldest child takes on the role of the parent while the parent is at work or at play.

The Bible does not tell us if there were other children in the home, but it does tell us of Leah and Rachel. Leah perhaps did not want to be an old maid and she went along with the program because she may have thought this has to be better than being alone. So Leah did not say a word while Jacob was making love to her. This one act created an attachment to him.

Why do some women get attached the moment intercourse takes place? I believe it is because women are emotional beings and this intimate act bonds the physical with the emotional. Men can go on to the next woman and continue on and on without any emotional attachment for this is their makeup. Is God a cruel God? Of course He isn't. That is why He tells us to "Flee fornication." (I Corinthians 6:18). We are to run from it because there is a bonding that takes place regardless of whether you want to acknowledge it or not. This bonding is the reason so many women stay in abusive situations. Yes, he may be physically and/or emotionally beating her up, but at least she is not alone.

Women are now attached even if they do not want to be. Most often women mistake lust for love and they settle for lust because they do not know the difference. When a woman has intercourse with a man, she has now bonded with him physically and emotionally. Because of this deep bond she will continue in sin. He gets what he wants from the relationship and she in turn lives in the hope of one day he will truly love her.

All Leah was doing was obeying her father and this act of obedience caused her to go through a season of rejection, loneliness and despair.

After some time Jacob married Rachel and they all lived together under one roof. Being in the house with her sister, she watched Rachel receive the love that she so desired. Can you imagine how you would feel in this situation? Think about it, watching this behavior seven days a week, 24 hours a day. That had to be something to behold, seeing it with your eyes and feeling it with your heart.

Looking at Leah, we see that she was not pretty to look upon. She was the other sister. You know the one - the homely one, the one who never gets to go out on any dates because of her looks, the one that people say is really sweet. They never say that she is pretty, only that she is really sweet. She may be the plain sister, the one with short hair or the one who is slightly overweight, the one that is crying out to be loved, the one who feels abandoned and alone.

I can relate to Leah because I was the other sister, the Leah. I was the one who was really sweet, the overweight one, the plain one. I watched my friends in envy, while their high school boyfriends walked them to their classes and carried their books. With all of the boys in school, I could not understand why none of them wanted to do the same for me. There were times when guys would try to talk to me and I was excited until they made passes and tried to touch my body inappropriately. When I told them no, they moved on and there I was again, all alone.

There was not much change after I graduated. I was still called sweet and I was still all alone. However, I did meet the man of my dreams, Jesus Christ. He was wonderful, but I still missed having someone to love me.

The Lord saw that Leah was hated so he opened her womb. The Lord saw Leah and the Lord sees you. My unmarried sister, God sees your pain and your loneliness. He sees how you are passed up because of your size, your skin color and maybe even the way you style your hair. Do you know that the Bible states that we are fearfully and wonderfully made? This is found in Psalm 139:14; the psalmist realized this to the point that he even gave God praise. But you know, sometimes in your darkest hour the Word of God may not even help. The Word does not help because you become so focused on the fact that you do not have anyone to hold your hand; or to hold you period. So, the Word of God, which is quick, sharp and powerful, becomes just empty words. Like Leah, you cannot give God praise because your focus is all wrong.

I would hear that scripture, and commit it to memory. Then I would watch a romantic movie where the star was a small beautiful girl and I would cry and say, "Why do I have to be alone, why do I have to be the sweet one, why can't I be the beautiful one that all of the guys like and want to be with, why do I have to be a Leah"? I would go through all of this because my focus was off. My precious sister, you must change your focal point to Jesus, who is there all of the time, loving and caring for you. He created you and He says that you are BEAUTIFUL!

You may be reading this book and thinking that this is only for sisters who are single and still looking for love. This book is for every woman who has ever felt like Leah.

Leah is the one that takes care of the house, the children and does her wifely duties, with no satisfaction from her husband. After he is done making himself happy in the marriage bed and not caring if you are or not, he gets up and goes for the remote control to watch television or goes on with his business. There you are in bed thinking to yourself, "Is this all there is? I did not sign up for this. I was just doing what I thought was the will of God."

These are the times when you must focus on God and pray for a change to come. Some men just do not understand what women need. Then there are even those men who do not care what women need as long as their needs are fulfilled. In both cases you must pray and ask God for guidance. He may lead you to pray for and or lead you to talk to your husband. Make sure the time is right.

As a godly wife, you still have to continue on with your duties as the wife, through the tears and all. I Peter 3:1, 2 says, *"Likewise, ye wives, be in subjection to your own husbands; that, if any obey not the word, they also may without the word be won by conversation of the wives: while they behold your chaste conversation coupled with fear."* This scripture is telling us to be in subjection to our own husband. If your husband is not obeying the Word of God, not living for God, or backslidden, you can win him by the way you carry yourself. You can win him by your walk, your actions, your talk, by still respecting and loving him. If this is where you are, I realize that it is not a piece of cake. Know that you can do all things through Christ who strengthens you according to Philippians 4:13.

There may be times when you just have to cry it out and that is okay. Tears are not signs of weakness. After you are done crying, pick yourself up, talk to your Heavenly Father and let Him strengthen you so that you can go on with your day.

What Leah went through is what women and even some men have gone through throughout the ages and that is rejection.

There are many different definitions for the word rejection and I would like to share some of them with you. Webster's online dictionary states a lot of different things about the words rejected and rejection.

To reject something or someone means to refuse to accept, agree to, believe in, or make use of something, e.g. because it is not good enough or not the right thing. Jacob refused to accept Leah and rejected her because she was not the right thing or the right person. When you refuse to accept something this means you have a choice in the matter. So he could have chosen to love her, but he chose not to. He obviously felt that she was not good enough to receive his love because the scripture states that she was hated. (Genesis 29:31)

Dear Sister, who in your life has told you that you were not good enough? Who told you you were not the right one? Who has rejected you? Was it the man who you forsook your family and friends for and now he has left you? Was it the man who told you that he loved you and would always be there for you and now someone told you that he was getting married to someone else?

Rejection brings a lot of pain, darkness, sadness and isolation. You feel as though you are all by yourself on this earth. You believe that no one knows what you are going through because you are the only one who has ever experienced this place. I want you to know that you are not the only one; there are ladies all over this world who are in the same position as you are, needing and wanting so badly to be accepted.

Rejection does not just come from a boyfriend or husband. It can come from a parent, a child, a family member, a long time friend who no longer speaks to you.
Another meaning of the word rejected is to behave in an unkind and unfriendly way toward somebody who expects or has a right to expect love, kindness, and friendship. As a child, parent, lover or spouse we expect to be loved. We do not expect to be rejected by a "loved one." We experience that from outsiders, but when we are rejected by those who are supposed to love us, be kind to us, be our friend; this is when it really hurts. You say to yourself, "How can you reject me Mom, when you took care of me for nine months in your womb and now you do not want to love me? Is it because I do not look the way you expected me to look? Is it because I look like my dad and because he rejected you, now when you see me you see him, and I have to suffer for it"?

How can your best friend from childhood decide that she no longer wants to be your friend? You know the one - she helped you make your first snowman, the one who used to play with dolls together; the one whom you shared all your secrets with. You two were inseparable, when people saw one; they always saw the other one too. How could she now reject you when you were always there for her? It just does not seem right, but it takes place every day.

To just throw something away is another definition for rejected. To throw away a relationship, a friendship, a marriage, to discard it like you throw away a piece of paper because it no longer meets your standards and you consider it unsuitable.

When two people get married, they make the vows in the sight of God and in the sight of men. The happy couple repeats the vows after the minister and say, "for better or for worst, in sickness and in health, until death do us part," vows that are made to last a lifetime. Somewhere along the line one decides that the other is no longer meeting their standards. They were on the same page when they first got married, but things have changed and instead of saying, "until death do us part" they should have said, "as long as you are meeting my standards."

I am sure that when Jacob woke up and saw Leah next to him, he just discarded her like an old shoe. Remember he told his father-in-law that he had tricked him or in other words, he had done him wrong. All he wanted to do was to get the wife he worked for and loved and it definitely was not Leah.

Once again let us revisit the meaning of the name Leah: weary. This lets us know that not only did she have to deal with being married to someone who did not love her and seeing her sister receive the love she so desired, but every time someone called her name they were calling her, "weary, tired, worn out, exhausted, drained." She had a lot to deal with even though she did not cause it herself.

What about you my precious sister, are you dealing with some issues that you did not cause yourself? Are you dealing with the pain and hurt from being rejected and are asking God why do you have to deal with this? Know that God will cause even what you are experiencing right now to work together for your good. Just hold on and allow these words to minister to you.

Rejection

I am not alone in what I am feeling
For people have felt this all over this land,
But it still does not make things any easier
What is needed is in such great demand.

Rejection is what I am experiencing
A pain that hurts so deep within,
Even though God is here and He knows it
In His love is where healing will begin.

CHAPTER TWO

JUST LOVE ME

"Surely the Lord hath looked upon my affliction; now therefore my husband will love me." (Genesis 29:32)

The Lord opened Leah's womb and she had a son, whom she named Reuben. (Genesis 29:32) According to this scripture, she thought that by having a son, Jacob would now love her; for she named her son Reuben which means, "behold a son."

Wow a Son! Aren't fathers so proud when they have sons? They even say 'son' in a special way. The sons are the ones who carry on the family name, the lineage; they are representations of the father. So here Leah produced a son and she just knew that now Jacob would love her.

The Lord saw Leah in her condition, the fact that she wanted to be loved. The Lord saw me in my condition and He also sees you in yours. Leah called her condition an affliction (isn't that something.) When I think of the word affliction, I think of sickness. I do not think of being married to a man that does not love you as an affliction, but this is what Leah called it.

Synonyms for the word affliction are: pain, misery, hardship, suffering, trouble, difficulty, burden, and problem. Leah did not ask for this! The scripture does not state anywhere that Leah wanted to marry Jacob or that he loved her or that he wanted to marry her. His heart belonged to Rachel. Leah was just minding her own business and this became her lot in life. Aren't you glad that you do not have to be forced to marry someone because your parents arranged it for you?

Sometimes people end up marrying because the woman is pregnant and the man wants to "do the right thing." Is it really doing the right thing if love is not in the picture? If we returned to the laws that were written in the book of Leviticus, and enforced them today, I believe there would be a lot less out of wedlock pregnancies and maybe even a lot less divorces.

The Lord saw Leah's pain, her suffering, her hardship, her burden and her difficulty. Let's look at her pain.

Leah was hurting because she was not receiving love from her husband. She was married and the husband is supposed to love the wife. That's what the Bible says. Why couldn't he love her or why didn't he love her? I believe that Jacob could not love Leah because he was in love with Rachel and that is where his focus was. Leah had to see that and it caused her great anguish.

There are women today all across the world whose husbands are still in love with their previous wives or their first loves and yet they married them. It is sad, but in a lot of cases it is the truth.

Leah was suffering because marriage is a union between you and your husband. It is not supposed to be you, your husband and his other wife. She suffered from rejection and it is a horrible thing to be rejected by your spouse. The two of you are supposed to become one. You want to cuddle and he does not, you want to talk and he does not, everyone around you is complimenting you but he is oblivious of the fact that you have on a new dress or that you have lost ten pounds. There are times when you want to make love and he does not. The Bible says that your husband's body belongs to you just like your body belongs to him, but in a lot of marriages this is a one way street.

A burden is something that you carry around and it weighs you down. The fact that Leah had to see Jacob and Rachel cuddling and toying with one another, knowing that was not taking place in her life, was something that she carried around in her mind. She had to deal with the fact that she was the door prize and that this was all a set up as she watched her sister experience happiness in the same house that she lived in. She said, "Surely the Lord has seen my affliction and now my husband will love me." Now he will cuddle and toy with me. Now he will sit with his arms around me as I hold our son. Now he will tell me how much he loves me. Leah just wanted to be loved by her husband. She had to experience loneliness even though she was married. She experienced emptiness because she was in an environment that was not fulfilling for her. The need to be loved was not being met by her husband.

Jacob did not love Leah, although he still had sex with her. Isn't that interesting? How many times has that happened in your life? Sometimes it can happen for years. Sometimes it happens just because a man wants to add another notch on his belt. There is healing for you if you were the victim in either of these situations. God is here to heal away the pain; He just wants to love you. Please let Him love you.

I wanted to be loved so badly that I was looking for love in all of the wrong places, so much so that I ended up engaged to a convicted criminal while he was in prison. I know that you may be saying to yourself, "You have got to be kidding me?" Well, I am not kidding.

A friend of mine said that she had a cousin in prison who needed someone to write to him and encourage him about Jesus because he had just given his life to the Lord. So I said, here I am, I can do that. I was newly saved and ready to win and counsel the world. Before I go on, let me tell you that writing to the opposite sex while they are in prison is not a healthy thing to do. Make sure you clear this with God and your pastor before you begin or you could end up in a mess.

So here I was, writing and getting to know this man. Encouraging him to read his Bible and pray, you know the religious things to do. It began with just letters and then it led to phone calls, visits and an engagement. Once he was released, we began dating and spending time together on a regular basis even though he did not go to church with me. I met his parents and he met mine. After all we were going to get married.

When he came home, he was not thinking about God. He just wanted to do his own thing, but I did not care because I had someone who loved me, or so I thought. He was a gentleman in the sense that he agreed with me to wait until we got married before we made love and I was happy about that. God was not too happy with this relationship, but you all know when you are in love, you do not care much about what anybody thinks. Not even God.

So, my Heavenly Father just let me go on in this foolishness until one day I received a phone call on my job. The caller told me that if my fiancé came to pick me up, not to get into his car because his parents have called and said that he had stolen a car and the police were after him. If I was in the car, they would have taken me to jail too. Thank God for His amazing Grace!

Keep in mind that throughout all of this time I just wanted to be loved. I was saved, sanctified and filled with the Holy Spirit, and yet I did not realize that all I needed was the Lord. Jesus was my Savior and Redeemer. I did not grasp the fact that He wanted to be my Lover, my Friend, and my Companion too. I did not understand that He was with me all of the time. I was looking outward instead of inward. It took some time, but I finally got there.

To my single sisters - please enjoy your season of just you and the Lord. It comes without interruption from a mate. It is a wonderful season, so take pleasure in loving the Lord, being in His presence and being intimate with Him. Let Him speak sweet nothings in your ear which are truths that you will value all of your days.

It is important to know that when God has called you out of darkness and has translated you into His marvelous light (I Peter 2:9); the enemy does not like it. The enemy will use your weaknesses to get you back into darkness. That is why you must deal with them and die to them or they will mess you up and cause serious embarrassment.

I learned some things from being engaged to a prisoner, but it did not stop me from wanting to be loved and held by another.

One day while seeking the Lord, He gave me this scripture: *"Simon, Simon, Satan has desired to have you that he may sift you as wheat; but I have prayed for you that your faith fail not and when thou art converted, thou will strengthen thy brethren."* (Luke 22:31, 32) I did not know what that meant nor did I understand what God was trying to tell me. I did not seek Him to find out what He meant either, which was a big mistake.

One night after leaving Bible Study I met this young man. He was not that great to look at, he did not have a job or a car, but he paid me some attention. Next thing you know, I was deeply involved with this man. Before I knew it, he had moved into my house and my virginity was gone. I was severely attached and in a horrible pit. I was still going to church and going through the motions as if nothing had changed. I was not lonely anymore, but now I was in a backslidden state and had to make a decision if I wanted a right relationship with God or if I wanted a wrong relationship with this man.

The Bible says in Numbers 32:23, *"Be sure, your sin will find you out,"* and that is exactly what happened.

My body was going through some changes and I did not understand what was going on so I made a doctor's appointment. That day is still so clear in my mind as if it were yesterday. The day of my appointment I remember being in my bedroom getting ready. I put on a black and red striped knit shirt with black pants. I was standing in front of my chest of drawers and I heard these words being sung so clearly, "Yes, Jesus loves me, yes, Jesus loves me, yes, Jesus loves me for the Bible tells me so." This song rang in my spirit and I just started crying. Jesus was letting me know that He still loved me even though I was in a mess. I am sure that you have guessed by now what the doctor had to say. I was four months pregnant and you should have seen me. I was a basket case. How was I going to tell my parents, my family, and my church family that I was pregnant?

Here I was, the apple of my father's eye, Daddy's little girl, and I am pregnant. I was an honor roll student, the one that was going to college to make something of myself and now I was pregnant. I have to tell you that even though I was 20 years old, living on my own, taking care of myself, I was still afraid to tell my mother because I thought she was going to kill me. What a day that was when I told her. She was so hurt, so disappointed in me, I had let her down. My family could not believe it because I was "in the church" attending every service and they just knew this would never happen to me. I had vowed that this would never happen to me. I thought it may happen to everyone all around me, but never to me. I Corinthians 10:12 states, *"Wherefore let him that thinketh he standeth take heed lest he fall."*

Now remember, there was still another group of people that I had to tell - my church family. That was so hard because I was being a hypocrite going through the motions. I was living in sin and I still held positions in the church. You can be so messed up, living in sin and still hold a post in the local church. You may fool the people, but you never fool God. No one condemned me, they just loved me. Of course I had to relinquish the positions that I held, but I still attended church faithfully even though I still had that man, my son's father, living in my house.

I was soul-tied or attached to my son's father. I felt like I could not do any better. I was in such a horrible pit and I thought there was no way I could ever get out; the only thing I knew was that I was no longer lonely. After I had a son, a year later I had a daughter.

I just wanted to be loved. Here I was a single parent with two children and then I found out I was not the only woman in this man's life.

Later on I discovered that there were others out there, but at least I had a part of him. How crazy is that? You do not think it is crazy when you are lonely and have low self- esteem. At least you have someone's attention some of the time.

When you want to be loved, you will settle for anything. You will settle for the drinker, the smoker, the cheater, and the unsaved. Even when you know that the Bible tells you not to be yoked together with an unbeliever. (II Corinthians 6:14) I know that refers to marriage, but I believe it also means relationships. If you are dating an unsaved man, you are going to compromise your commitment with Christ in one way or another.

God gave me two beautiful children out of that relationship and I am glad to say that they are serving God, but that was not the proper way. There is a more excellent way. Please take my advice and ask God to give you a manifestation of His love. He will love you like no other.

The song that comes to mind is Love Lifted Me, written by James Rowe and Howard E. Smith. When nothing else could help love lifted me. That is my theme song because that is what brought me out - God's love. He was there all of the time. He is there for you and when you feel like you want to be loved, just reach up and grab his love.

Now that I am converted, I am strengthening the brethren and that includes you. Learn from my mistakes and do not allow yourself to make the same mistakes I did. Even if you have already, it is not too late for you to turn around, stop what you are doing and ask God to get you out of the relationship. If you are serious, God will help you get out of it. God sent that man out of my house when I got serious about wanting to be free and wanting to serve God in righteousness. You must love God more than that man or relationship because that ungodly connection is serious and it is not easily disconnected. God sent my sister and a friend to move in with me and to help me. It was as if that man had disappeared from the face of the earth. I am so glad that God is the God of a second chance and I am so thankful for His love towards me!

Two song writers wrote the following songs. If you know them, stop and sing them and let the Lord minister to you right where you are:

> "Jesus loves me this I know, for the Bible tells me so. Little ones to him belong, they are weak, but He is strong. Yes, Jesus loves me. Yes, Jesus loves me. Yes, Jesus loves me for the Bible tells me so." (Written by Anna B. Warner)

> "I don't know why Jesus loves me. I don't know why He cares. I don't know why, He sacrificed His life. Oh, but I'm glad, I'm glad He did. Where would I be if Jesus didn't love me? Where would I be if He didn't care? Where would I be, if He hadn't sacrificed His life? Oh, but I'm glad, so glad He did!" (Written by Andréa Crouch)

These songs express who Jesus is. He is love. He loves us in spite of us. In spite of our ways, our rights and our wrongs, He just loves us. The Bible says that we love Him because He first loved us (I John 4:19).

It is a hard thing to grasp that Jesus loves us no matter what, because His love is not earthly love. Earthly love can change with the wind. Today a person can love you and tomorrow when they wake up, they can decide not to love you any longer, but Jesus never changes. His love never fails and His love never alters so He loves us all day, every day. He does not love the sin that we find ourselves in, but He still loves us.

Leah wanted to be loved by Jacob and she did not know there was a greater love that existed for her and that all she had to do was receive it. I am sure that when she realized that Jacob still did not love her in spite of her giving him a son that added more pain to what she was already experiencing. I believed that she just poured the love that she had and wanted into her baby boy Reuben in hopes that one day things would change.

Just Love Me

I have searched in so many places
Trying to find love from an earthly man,
I have compromised some of my standards
Just for a ring to be placed on my hand.

I have found what I thought was true love
Instead it was only just lust,
Lord you didn't condemn me at all
In your love I must learn how to trust.

CHAPTER THREE

THE LORD HEARS

"Because the Lord hath heard that I was hated, he hath therefore given me this son also." (Genesis 29:33)

First the Lord saw and now the Lord heard. What did he hear? The scripture tells us that He heard that Leah was hated. Who was talking and saying that Leah was hated? Did Jacob literally tell Leah that he hated her? I do not believe that. I believe that Rachel could have hated her and voiced it and God heard that.

Go with me if you will. Imagine yourself married and you are not the only wife. The other wife now has a son and you see your husband holding the son, but you do not have a son for him to hold, how would you feel? Rachel could have begun hating Leah for the simple fact that she had children and she herself was barren. If she was like one of the sisters that I know, she would have told Leah something like this, "You need to stop fooling yourself. Jacob loves me and he does not love you. You know that he worked all of those years for me. You were tricked into becoming his wife, but I was his wife by choice. Even though you are popping out those babies, I am the one that he loves so you can have all of the babies that you want, I will still have

his heart and he will never love you." This sounds almost like
a soap opera, but you better believe that someone was saying
something. It may not have been these exact words, but God
was hearing someone say that Leah was unloved.

Could it have been that Leah's family and friends saw how Jacob
treated her compared to how he treated Rachel and they said that
she was hated and this is what God heard?

Or, did Leah actually tell God that she was hated because this
was how she felt?

Night after night and day after day she could have been crying
out to God and saying "God you already see that I am unloved
by my husband. Look at how Jacob is treating me compared to
how he is treating my sister. People are talking about me and it
hurts so badly, please hear my cry and help me."

Everyone deserves to be loved and I am sure that Leah felt so
cold without the love that she so desired from her husband. This
was a hard pill to swallow and for the scripture to say that the
Lord heard that she was hated, someone was talking.

Have you ever felt like you were hated? Have you ever felt
like you had some type of disease because men did not give
you the time of day? They stayed away from you like you had
the plague. Well I did. I would talk to God and say things like,
"What is wrong with me God? Why do I have to be alone? Why
can't I even go out on a date? Why won't men give me a second
look?" I suppose it wasn't all men, because I did get second
looks from men who were out for one thing and also from men
who were a lot older than I was, but not anyone my age who
wanted God and a wife.

I wanted someone to love me for me, not someone to lust after my body, but someone to love me. I wanted commitment, not a one night stand.

God heard that Leah was unloved and he gave her another son and she named him Simeon which means God heard and was listening to her. So whenever she looked at her son she was saying, "God, you hear everything that is being said about me and You know that it is not right. You are listening to my cries and I know that one day things are going to change for me."

The Lord heard Leah and he hears you as well. All throughout Psalm 34 it talks about the Lord hearing and acting upon what He has heard.

Psalms 34 verse 6 states, *"This poor man cried, and the LORD heard him, and saved him out of all his troubles."* I believe what the Word of God says, that when we cry, He hears us and will save us out of all of our troubles. This scripture is not a quick fix; meaning that we cry today and our troubles are gone in a moment. This scripture just assures us that the Lord has heard and salvation, deliverance or whatever the need, it is on the way. The need may be to eradicate the loneliness that you are experiencing at this moment. The need may be to experience God's loving arms wrapped around you and letting you know that the change is on its way. When you cry God will move on your behalf. Let us look at another scripture to confirm what I am telling you.

Psalms 34 verse 15 states, *"The eyes of the LORD are upon the righteous, and his ears are open unto their cry."* Now there is a condition in this particular scripture for God's ears to be opened unto us. We must walk in righteousness. We must have a right relationship with God for Him to move on our behalf. We have a right to expect Him to move when we are walking in righteousness according to this scripture. His eyes are upon us, as we walk in righteousness and His ears our open to our cry.

Now we know that according to Isaiah 64:6 our righteousness is as filthy rags, but we have been made righteous because of Christ and this is the righteousness that we stand in by faith. So the Lord's ears are open to our cry. He hears us and He answers us and it does not matter what time of the day it is, He is always with us, He will always help us and He will always hear us.

Now in verse 17 of Psalms 34 the psalmist takes this a step deeper and states that not only does the Lord hear when the righteous cry, but He continues to hear every time they cry and He will deliver them each and every time out of all of their predicaments and difficulties. So in other words, if you are in right standing with God and living for the Lord and you are experiencing any type of difficulty in your life, the Lord hears you as you cry out to Him and He has promised to deliver you out of them all. You can stand on His word and His promises.

A difficult time is when you just had your heart broken because of someone telling you that they love you but left you for someone else. The Lord will deliver you out of the hurt and pain. A difficult time is when all of your friends are with their boyfriends and they are going to the movies or to the game and you are all alone. The Lord will deliver you from the feeling of being alone and replace that with His love and His presence. I am telling you that I know what I am talking about. I am not telling you something that I read in a book or watched on the television, I am telling you something that I have experienced. As I cry unto the Lord, He comes through with the supply to whatever need I have at that time.

He hears that you are not being loved the way you want to be and He sent His only begotten Son to die on the cross for you because He loves you so much. God wants to have a real relationship with you and before He sends you your mate, He wants to love you first and show you what real love is.

We cry out for love that no earthly man can give us, only God can. You see when we were born; we were born with a void that only God can fill. We will try other things to pacify the void like drugs, sex, men, food, you name it, but only God can fill the void. Even after you have these substitutes, you still feel empty because God is who you really need.

Like Leah, we all want to be loved. You see after Leah had the first son, that experience did not satisfy her because she was still unloved. In her state she could not praise God. Notice that Leah acknowledged the Lord, but could not give Him any praise. Remember the scriptures told us that the Lord hath heard, the Lord hath seen that she was unloved, but Leah could not give God any praise until after the fourth son. She was bitter and unhappy because she was thrown into a marriage. It does not seem like she had a choice; she had to be obedient to her father. In your state, can you praise God? Can you count your blessings and give God the glory right where you are? Or are you so in need of a man that you just cannot do it?

Are you married to a man who does not love you? Are you willing to stay in the marriage because you were serious about the vows that you spoke on your wedding day? I just want to tell you that nothing is too hard for God! The effectual fervent prayer of a righteous man (woman) will avail much. (James 5:16) Pray for your husband, walk in submission, and make sure that his clothes are cleaned, the house is clean and the children are well taken care of. Also make sure he has a good meal to eat

daily and that you keep yourself together. If God sees that you
are doing what you know to do, and your husband sees you as
well, things will change!

Now, if you are in a relationship where the man does not love you
and you are not married to him, talk to God. Ask your Heavenly
Father if this is your husband and if he is not, ask God for the
strength to get out of it. I know that I have already said this, but
it is important enough to be repeated. Do not settle for someone
who does not love you. Even if he is a Christian, he may not be
the husband for you. You do want the man who was meant to be
your husband, don't you?

God showed Leah that He loved her by blessing her with another
son. He demonstrates His love to you all of the time. He is the
one that breathes the breath of life in you. He is the one that
provides for you and takes care of all of your needs. God will
even take care of the need to be loved as long you allow Him to.
The Lord hears which lets us know that we must be careful with
our words. Proverbs 18:21 tells us that, *"Death and life are in
the power of the tongue and they that love it shall eat the fruit
thereof."* Also in Chapter 14 of Proverbs Solomon talks about
a wise woman builds her house but a foolish woman plucks
or tears it down with her hands. Even though you may not be
receiving the love from your husband that you deserve, you can
tear down your household by your actions and your words. Your
words have power and with your words you can create, just like
your Heavenly Father did when He created the heavens and the
earth. He just spoke the world into existence.

As godly wives, we must be careful how we speak about our
husbands; and to whom we speak to concerning our husbands.
Do not curse your husband, but lift him up and cover him.
Remember the scripture that says, *"Love covers a multitude*

of sins." (I Peter 4:8 New King James Version) He may not love you now like you want or deserve to be loved, but as you continue to pray and speak life into your marriage, things can and will change.

Sometimes I do not think that we realize the power that we have inside of us. We have the same power that raised Jesus from the dead living within. Ephesians 3:20 tells us that God is able to do exceeding abundantly above all that we can ask or think according to the power that works on the inside of us. This scripture lets us know that there is some serious power that is working on the inside of us. With this power, we can change situations and circumstances by declaring and praying.

Lord Hear Me

Lord, hear my cry for I need you
I need you to heal this heart of mine,
Heal me from the pain and hurt inside me
Heal me with your love that is so divine.

For you have seen all that I have been through
The loneliness, rejection and the shame,
In your voice there is such sweet assurance
I just need you to call me by my name.

CHAPTER FOUR

THE NEED FOR CONNECTION

"Now this time will my husband be joined unto me, because I have born him three sons..." (Genesis 29:34)

Here we go again...

I can imagine, Leah in a room, sweating, pushing, crying, going through labor to bring forth her third child. The midwife announces, "It is another boy!" Leah is smiling from ear to ear and she says, *"this time he will be joined to me."* What a statement. We do not know if this was the first thing she said after the baby was born, all we know is she said it. "This time" is what Leah said which meant that her husband was still not joined to her even though they were married.

You would think that after she had two sons, Reuben and Simeon, Jacob would be joined to her, but he was not.

My dear single sisters, just because you have one or more children with a man that you love, <u>please</u> do not think he is joined to you. For those of you who are in a relationship with a man and you want him as your own, please do not think that you are going to trap him by getting pregnant. That does not work. You get pregnant, have the child, he leaves and then you are stuck with raising your child or children alone until God unites you with someone else.

I see it all of the time. Women just want to be united with someone, so they get with the first man available, get pregnant, and then they think they have him all to themselves. I am speaking to you from experience. I was pregnant and living on one side of the street and just a few houses away on the other side of the street was another woman who was sleeping with my man. Years later I learned that someone else was carrying his child at the same time that I was. Look at the mess that I was in just wanting to be attached to someone.

I need to clarify something before I go on. I did not want to get pregnant; I just wanted to be loved. After I got pregnant I just knew that we were now a couple, that we were joined. I even wanted to marry this man because I was pregnant. I wanted to do the right thing by getting married, but he did not want to marry me. How do you think I felt then? Do you think I put him out of my house and moved on with my life? No, because I was not alone anymore, at least that is what I told myself.

Leah was married to someone who she was not joined to. How can this be? I thought that marriage was supposed to join a man and a woman together; at least that is what the marriage vows state. Why wasn't Leah joined to Jacob? Why was she separated from the man that she married? I know that she was not physically separated because they were still producing children, but emotionally she was separated. Being emotionally alone is a hurtful thing. Yes, he came to bed with her and yes, he had sex with her, but his heart was not with her.

Leah named this son Levi, which means connect. She was speaking what she wanted to see. She wanted to be connected to her husband, not just physically, but emotionally too. She wanted Jacob to love her just like she loved him. She thought that since she now had three sons he would join himself with her. After all, she was producing children for him and Rachel was not.

How many children do you have to have before you realize that the man you are with is not going to join himself to you? If he was, he would have put a ring on your finger and met you at the altar a long time ago. Wake up my sister and open your eyes to the truth. The truth is God wants to be connected with you more than you want to be connected to a man.

The reason Jacob was not joined to Leah was because he was joined to another; Rachel. I am speaking to those of you who are in a relationship with a married man; when are you going to realize that he is not going to leave his wife and marry you? Get out of that situation! You know that God is not pleased and you are keeping God from blessing you.

Wait on God. He will give you the desires of your heart and bless you with a mate that will love you, be in love with you and take good care of you. Notice that I said he will love you and be in love with you. These are two different things and we as women want both. I believe we need both.

To love someone means to be committed to that person for the rest of your life. You will walk in forgiveness and cover their faults; you will be longsuffering, kind and patient with that person. I am talking about your husband but this also applies to everyone that you love. To be in love with someone means you get excited when you are going to see him. You will do anything for him because he loves you and is in love with you. Your heart beats a little faster and you miss him when he is not around. He is the first face you want to see when you wake up in the morning and the last one that you want to see when you go to bed at night. Being in love means knowing that you have someone to walk with and hold your hand, someone who cares about you and is constantly on your mind. You do not want to do anything to upset them, but you want to please them always. To be joined means to be attached to, to be united, to be tied and it also means to be together.

Ask yourself this question, 'What am I attached too?' This is a question that only you can answer, because you are the one reading this book and you are the one that must examine yourself.   I am not here to judge you or condemn you, I am here to minister to you so that you can receive healing and be connected to whom God has chosen for your life.

Do you know that if you are attached to a man who is not a born again believer and you decide to marry him; your father in law would be the devil?

I counseled with a sister who told me that the Lord told her to marry this unsaved man. My thought was, "what is wrong with this picture?" Well first off, God will not tell us anything that will contradict His Word. The Bible clearly states, *"Be ye **not unequally yoked** together with unbelievers: for what fellowship hath righteousness with unrighteousness? And what communion hath light with darkness"?* (II Corinthians 6:14) So how can the two, as man and wife, fellowship when he is in darkness and you are in light. The two cannot agree. To have a good marriage takes work, it does not just happen. But if you go into the marriage already on two different sides, that will make the work twice as difficult.

If we do not allow God to send us our mate, we will end up with some attachments or connections that have consequences we never would have thought possible.

Here is just a small list of some of the things that we have joined ourselves to on our journey of being loved…

Bisexuals or the new name for it is "the down low brothers" – these men have decided that they want to be married, but they also want to express themselves sexually with another man without their wife knowing anything about it. You talk about something being sent straight from the pit of hell! This is taking place in our day and age. Once the wife finds out, she is devastated and her life is broken into thousands of pieces. God can mend the broken pieces and put them back together again, but it takes time and it causes the women so much pain.

Some women who cannot say no to their fleshly lusts have connected themselves to AID's carriers. I just heard on the news that some men who are HIV positive are having unprotected sex with women, spreading the disease and not even telling the women that they have it. This is now a felony and they can go to prison. I am sure the women are not concerned about prison but about their life expectancy. Wanting to be joined to somebody has now cost her, her life.

What about the man who is so involved with his church and God that he has completely left you out of the picture except when the lights go out? I am talking about the man that you thought

the Lord sent to you.   He is a man of God.   He loves the Lord
with all of his heart.   He holds a position in the local church.
He did and said all of the right things and no one had anything
bad to say about him prior to your marriage.   You fell in love
with him and he was in love with you until after you said, "I
do."   On your honeymoon night he made passionate love to you
all night and you were in marital bliss.   The next day you wake
up and he wants to pray and have a nice Bible study together.
How wonderful is this until you realize this is all he wants to do.
He spends a lot of time on his cell phone checking on things at
church making sure everything is taken care of.   You talk about
going out to a movie and dinner and he is too holy for movies
and just wants to read his Bible after dinner.   Bro. Smith now
needs him to assist him with some work that needs to be done at
the church and he is gone for a few hours.   He comes home and
you want to spend some quality time with him and he now needs
to go and pray. This seems unreal, but this does happen.

Now let us talk about the drug addicts that women have joined
themselves to and in a lot of cases, the woman did not even
know that there was a problem. The addict has been clean now
for several months, he is going to church, having fellowship
with the brethren and God has blessed him with a good job.
Things are going on just fine. This is the happy ending to a lot
of marriages, but in some this is not the case.

One day the taste for the drug begins to resurface in his mouth or
in his thoughts and he has to go and get the drug. He cannot just
get high one time, he now has to make up for lost time.   Now
that he is addicted again, he is either late for work or skipping
work altogether. After a while his inconsistencies causes him
to get fired. With no job and the need for the drug he has to do
something. He begins lying to his family and friends to get drug
money. After he has used them all up, he begins to sell things

from his home. Things that belong to his wife and his children; he is hurting the ones he loves but it doesn't matter. The need for the drugs is so strong. The drug has taken the place of the wife and she is no longer united with him because he is united or tied up to the drugs. But she is still connected to him because she loves him.

Just wanting to be attached to someone has caused some women to marry men who are slothful. These are the men who do not want to work or go to school to better themselves. They just want you to take care of them like you were their mother. These brothers enjoy the good life. They enjoy their wives doing all of the cooking, and the cleaning as well as going off to work every day. They enjoy sitting at home in front of the television watching sports or playing video games. They have no motivation to do anything. Some of them have come from a background where their fathers did the exact same thing.

My Apostle always says, "When God created man, before he gave him a wife, he gave him a job!" And this is the truth! I can see if something is physically wrong with the man and this keeps him from working, but if he is in good health he can go to work. He can work inside the home by starting his own business or he can work outside the home, but he must put laziness aside and do something. And if you are connected to someone like this and you are afraid to tell him this, you can have him call me and I will tell him for you.

There are a lot of men in this world who are abusers. Some are physical abusers and some are verbal abusers. Some women have become attached to them because they did not see the signs when they were dating. "Everyone gets mad sometimes and as long as I do not make him mad, I will not have to see that side of him again." One time becomes several times, one hit becomes several beatings. You are not his child and he has no business putting his hands on you. If you are in an abusive situation, there is help available for you. There is a Domestic Violence Hotline in your area. If you cannot find the number; call information because you were not put on this earth to be someone's whipping post. You were put on this earth to be loved.

Verbal abuse is worst than physical abuse. Words do harm you in spite of what the childhood rhyme says. Words leave scars, unlike physical scars; they hurt inwardly and cause an effect to take place emotionally. Verbal abusers like to use words and phrases like, "stupid, ugly, worthless, fat, 'no one wants you', 'you cannot do anything right', 'get out of my face you disgust me'." When you hear words like this, know that this is the devil talking. He is the father of lies and you can counteract every word by saying the opposite even if you have to do it under your breath. My dear sister, do not keep being abused because you want to stay connected, you are worth so much more than this!

What about being connected to a man who is extremely loving and the epitome of how a man is to treat a woman one day and then the next day becomes the very spawn of hell. He works and has a very good job, buys you all kinds of unexpected gifts, and things are going really well. This makes you happy and you fall in love with him. Then things change. He gets angry at the drop of a hat; he yells and throws things. You sit quietly, not knowing what else he is going to do. Some women become so attached to men like this, that they do not want to leave. Because when he is at his best behavior he is buying gifts and loving them in such a way that they have never experienced before. They feel that the good days far outweigh the bad. For his anger is not geared toward them so they feel that every thing is fine and they can handle this type of relationship.

In the midst of wanting to be connected to her husband Leah had a connection to God with her son Levi. The priests, who were responsible for the Tabernacle, came from the tribe of Levi. They were responsible for performing the daily sacrifices in the Tabernacle, they maintained the Tabernacle and they counseled the people on how to follow God. They were the peoples' representatives before God and they had to live holy and sanctified lives. What an honor for Leah for her child to bring forth the priesthood in the midst of what she was going through, God had a plan.

We as women have the need to be joined, attached to or tied to someone unless we have the gift of celibacy. God ordained it for one man to be joined to one woman which is the proper setting for children to be born. As women of God, we must seek God and as we do so, God will direct the right man into our lives and we will be the good thing that he has found, according to the scripture. (Proverbs 18:22)

We just need to seek God with our whole heart and live for Him and when the time is right the man will come. We do not have to seek out the man. Let me say that again… we do not have to seek out the man.

Sometimes women do not want to wait for God. They take matters into their own hands and end up with a big mess. Sisters, if you wait on the Lord, He will give you the right one, I assure you!
So until that day comes, join yourself, be attached to, and tied to Jesus Christ! Stick to Him like glue and when you do, nothing will be able to get between the two of you unless He gives the okay.

I Need Attachment

Attachment was all that I was after
Being the rib from somebody's side,
For Eve was made from the rib of Adam
And by his side she knew she was to abide.

I only want to be joined with
The one that the Father has for me,
So I will keep my relationship with Him
Trusting in His Word continually.

CHAPTER FIVE

WHAT ME HAS DONE TO ME
"What is man (woman) that thou art mindful of him? ..."
(Psalms 8:4)

You may be saying to yourself "what is this chapter doing in this book. After all, this book is about people who have hurt us and rejected us, right"? True enough there were some people that have hurt us and we must get over that pain and rejection, but what about what we have done to our own bodies, and emotions. What have we allowed to fester and grow inside of us? This is what I want to bring to light.

We have allowed certain things like depression, anxiety, stress, negative thoughts and negative words, to enter into our spirits. Now we must get free of those things in order for us to move on in life and in our Christian journey.

Let's take a moment and look at depression. I must admit that I am not an expert on depression, but I do know that it is the opposite of happiness. It is the state of being sad and hopeless. There are times when depression has tried to take hold of my life, but I refused to let it. This lets me know that I had a choice in the matter. I had the choice of dwelling on what made me sad or dwelling on the goodness of the Lord and I chose the latter. When a person is without hope they may turn to pills, alcohol or drugs, but with Christ we do not have to do this. We do not have to dwell in sadness or hopelessness because God gives us faith which is the substance of things hoped for. So we have hope because we are in Christ. We have a hope that goes beyond the grave for we know that once we leave this life, we will go to be with the Lord and live with Him eternally.

There are those who have allowed anxiety and stress to take hold of their minds and now they cannot function without a pill. They need a pill to wake up and then another pill to go to sleep. Philippians 4:6 states, *"Be careful for nothing; but in every thing by prayer and supplication with thanksgiving let your requests be made known unto God."* Another word for careful is anxious; so what the writer is telling us in this verse is not to worry about anything, but take everything to God in prayer and thank Him in advance for the answers. Again, we have a choice. We can choose to worry about what is going on around us, the circumstances and situations of life or we can give them to God in prayer and let Him handle it all; for He is well able to do so.

I am sure that while reading this book you have remembered that I was engaged to a man while he was in prison. You may have even asked yourself, "Why would a born again Christian woman get engaged to a man who was still in prison"? Please do not take this the wrong way, because nothing is wrong with prisoners. We all have done things in our lives; which only by God's grace and mercy spared us from serving time in prison. Jesus is able to cleanse and deliver the hardest of hearts and turn them around. Nothing is too hard for our God. Jesus died for all and His blood cleanses us all from unrighteousness, but this was not the will of God for my life. I was engaged to this man because I suffered from low self esteem. I was not the woman who could get any man she desired; I was just the plain Jane. Finally when someone paid some attention to me I thought that was my only choice.

Some of us have allowed the world to dictate how we are supposed to look, how we are supposed to act and what size we are supposed to be. We are to be in this world, because we live here, but not of the world. Meaning the world should not be dictating to us, but we need to dictate to the world. We are to be shining lights that reaches out and causes men and women to want what we have. We need to be trend setters and not the other way around.

While standing in the checkout line at the grocery store, we are bombarded by magazines with super models on the cover. Their bodies are always a perfect 10; no blemish and not fat. Then as we leaf through the pages we see articles with guaranteed strategies for weight loss: "10 Super Foods for Super Weight Loss results", "7 Foods to avoid for quick weight loss", "Wonder Pills – Lose 10 pounds in 3 Days!" I don't know about you, but that is the magazine that I want to buy. I want to take the wonder pill so that I can look like the supermodel. After all, everyone notices her in a positive way and no one is making fun of her. I ordered the wonder pills, $40.00 plus shipping and handling, which was not in my budget. With anticipation I started the "Wonder Pill Weight Loss Program". I took the pills, restricted certain "forbidden" foods and the weight came off. My money and my enthusiasm were in scarce supply, so I stopped the program. As you may have guessed, I not only gained the weight I lost, but some additional pounds as well. Has this ever happened to you? You may have not taken the wonder pill, but what about all of the fad diets that have come out through the years? What **me** has done to me has affected my natural body. Trying to lose weight with fad diets is not healthy nor is it wise. We must forgive ourselves from causing pain to our own bodies. In their quest to look like a super model, some have ended up causing irreversible damage to their digestive system.

I just want to make sure you understand that we do have a choice in the matter as to what and how we eat. There are some people who have food addictions as well as eating disorders. I am not talking to those people at this time. I am only talking to those who make decisions on a daily basis concerning what foods and how much of those foods to eat.

There are times when we eat because we are depressed, sad, or lonely. We have become emotional eaters and this is not wise either. I find it interesting that we use food for everything. When a baby is born we eat, when someone dies we eat, when someone gets married we eat, when we have a meeting we eat. These special occasions are times to eat, but sometimes at these events we eat more than we should and that's not good for our bodies. Food is for our nourishment and it keeps us alive. We are not to become friends with food, nor do we live to eat. When you find yourself eating and you know that you are not hungry, you need to ask yourself, "Why am I eating this? Am I eating to fulfill some type of need?" God is the one who is to fulfill our needs and we need to allow Him to do so.

So I ended up engaged to someone in prison because I did not feel like I had any self worth. I also thought this type of life was what I deserved and that I could not do any better. Not thinking highly of yourself will make you settle. It will make you settle and think that you do not deserve anything better. It will even make you think that all you deserve is a man who does not work and that your job is to take care of him.

Low self worth will also cause you to stay in a relationship when a man is cheating on you, even though you are not married to him. It will make you feel that no one else will want you and you will end up alone. So you put up with him having relationships outside of yours because you do not want to be alone. If this is you, look at what you are doing to yourself and realize that you do not have to stay in this relationship.

Negative words have an effect on us as well. There are some who have heard disapproval all of their lives. Negative words like stupid, ugly and fat enter into your spirit man and beat you down and create illusions in your subconscious that appear to be real. For we are daughters of the most High God; we are not those negative things at all. Since we have allowed those things to enter in we settle for ..... (You fill in the blank).

As I mentioned before in Chapter Three, death and life are in the power of the tongue. Our words have power; words can have a positive or negative effect in our life. Even though we have the ability to cast down every word that comes against the knowledge of the truth, we do not, which in turn affects our self worth. We do not have to receive negativity in our lives from anyone. The truth of the matter is we are blessed and highly favored of the Lord and God thinks very highly of us!

The word esteem means to value something or someone highly. Some synonyms for this word are: appreciate, prize, cherish and hold dear. So, if you are a person with low self -esteem it means that you do not think highly of yourself. You do not appreciate or cherish yourself and therefore since you do not, you do not think anyone else does either. When you have low self - esteem, you believe when negative things happen to you, it is what you deserve. We must deal with this low value of ourselves.

Jesus tells us in Luke 10:27, *"And He answering said, Thou shalt love the Lord thy God with all thy heart, and with all thy soul, and with all thy strength, and with all thy mind; and thy neighbor as thyself."* This is a commandment from the Lord and this command is telling us that we are to love Him and then we are to love our neighbor as we love ourselves. But if you do not think highly of yourself or even love yourself, how can you walk in obedience to this scripture?

You need to understand that you need to love yourself. That is where my problem was and I did not grasp it. Yet, I was popular in school and everyone respected me. Teachers talked about what a pleasure I was to have in class. People wanted to be around me because I made them laugh and I too loved to laugh. I laughed to cover up the fact that I did not like myself. I did not value myself. I was miserable inside.

I was engaged to a man who was locked up, and did not have a plan for his life; no dreams or goals. He wasn't going anywhere with his life and as long as I was with him, I wasn't going anywhere either. I just wanted to be loved and I did not have any self-worth. I felt that he was the best that God had for me. You see when you do not think very much of yourself, you blame God for situations or things that He does not have anything to do with. God did not want me engaged to this man. Looking back over that situation, I can see now that God was not in that at all. When the time is right for marriage, number one, the man should be a born again believer, and number two, he should have a j-o-b! In the Garden of Eden, before God gave Adam a wife, he gave Adam a job and that is the proper order.

You can have it going on, you can have your PHD and an excellent career, your body in excellent condition and still suffer with low self-esteem. You see, it is nothing on the outside of you that makes the difference; it is what is on the inside of you. Even then, you must realize who is on the inside of you, and that who is Jesus Christ.

When you allow negative thoughts to enter into your spirit and you constantly put yourself down, when you get married, those thoughts will actually keep you from receiving the benefits of a happy marriage. We are to enjoy our mates and want to be with him and it should not be a struggle to receive his love. God has given us a choice in this life. We can choose to sit around and feel sorry for ourselves because of what others have done to us, or because of what we have done to ourselves or we can pick ourselves up, get into the Word of God, get our deliverance and get free.

Another thing that we have allowed to happen to us that we need to get free from is allowing people to dump on us. What I mean is people think because we are nice and sweet it gives them the right to just dump all of their garbage on us. They are having a bad day, someone hit their car, someone took their parking space, whatever has happened to them, and then they call you on the phone and hold up your time just spewing out all of this stuff in your ear. Some even call you to talk about the happenings of the church that they disagree with. Once you do get off of the phone, you are now weighed down and sometimes even depressed by the conversation that you had with them. You are not a trash dumpster and you need to tell that person or those people to bring you words of encouragement or do not call your phone. I am sure that you know exactly what I am talking about. Yes, we are to be good listeners and give advice to family and friends, but some people do not want your advice, but they want the opportunity to bring you down or tell you the latest gossip. Stop allowing this to happen. These words or conversations do not need to be a part of your daily diet and you have much to do for the Kingdom of Heaven. If you point them to the scriptures, I am sure they will stop dialing your number as often as they do.

My married sisters, there are some things that you must let go. Let go of the pain, the regrets, and the abuse to your own emotions and bodies, let it go. If you hold on to all of that mess it will make you think that you deserve to be beaten, you deserve to be taken for granted, and you deserve to be verbally abused. After all, your mother went through it and her mother did too. This is just how things are supposed to be. I want you to know it is a lie from the father of lies; the devil.

We deserve to be treated like queens. I am sure that before the fall in the Garden of Eden, Adam treated Eve with the utmost respect. Remember in Genesis, once he saw Eve, he declared, *"This is now bone of my bones and flesh of my flesh."* (Genesis 2:23) I am sure that he loved her with all of his heart and he demonstrated that love. I believe that he was excited about what the Lord had given him and he cherished her. That is exactly how marriages are supposed to be today.

Sometimes you can beat yourself up so badly that you just can not receive the love from your husband. He could be doing everything he can to make you happy and you can't respond. He can buy you flowers, take you out to dinner, tell you how beautiful you are, and you cannot receive it because you do not believe it.

What me has done to me has made you even stop looking at yourself in the mirror. There was a time in my life when I would look at myself because I had to make sure I did not leave any toothpaste on my face or that my hair was in place. And even then I would only look at my hair, not my face or my body, just my hair. I did not want to look to make sure my clothes looked right because I did not like myself and therefore I did not want to look at myself. I was so messed up because I did not look like the woman that everyone wanted to be with. But now I have a full length mirror and I check myself out often because I love myself and I am not ashamed of who God made me.

To my unmarried sisters, if you do not deal with what you have allowed to happen in your life, you will end up marrying someone who is not in love with you, someone who does not value you as his help mate. You will marry for the sake of being married. Get beyond the past mistakes and forgive yourself. Do not become bitter like Naomi in the book of Ruth.

Naomi experienced some terrible things in her life. There was a famine in her country so her husband took her and their two sons to another land. While they were there, her two sons got married. Something happened and her husband and sons died. She heard that the famine was over and she went back home with one of her daughter- in-laws. Bitter at what had happened to her, though no fault of her own; she could not see that God was still in her life and that He had a purpose for her.

Whatever you have done to yourself or have allowed to happen to you, please forgive yourself and get past it. Let the past be the past. This is a brand new day and God has so much in store for you.
You need to go to God and ask Him to deliver you from the things that you have done to yourself. He may lead you to someone to pray with you and by them praying for you, you can get free; or He may just lead you to some scriptures that can make you free. Meditating on the Bible is a powerful tool. By renewing your mind with the Word of God, you begin to realize who you are and who you are in Him.

Do you believe that Jesus would have died on the cross for you even if you were the only person on earth? If you do not or can not believe that, you are thinking too low of yourself. I want to share a scripture that will assist you in your thinking. Psalms 8:4-9,

> *"What is man that thou art mindful of him? And the son of man that thou visitest him? For thou hast made him a little lower than the angels, and hast crowned him with glory and honor. Thou madest him to have dominion over the works of thy hands; thou hast put all things under his feet: All sheep and oxen, yea, and the beasts of the fields; the fowl of the air and the fish of the sea, and whatsoever passeth through the paths of the seas. O Lord our Lord, how excellent is thy name in all the earth!"*

God is mindful of us. He has us on His mind. Think about this for a moment. The God of the universe, the God who created the heavens and the earth has us on His mind. If we were not worth anything, He would not have us on His mind. For God has crowned us with glory and honor. He has given us dominion over this earth because the earth is the work of His hands. Do you think that if we did not have any value, He would have done this? Absolutely not! We are somebody!

I Peter 2:9 tell us that we are a chosen generation, a royal priesthood, a holy nation and His own special people! We are God's very own people. That should make you excited to know that the God who holds the world in His hand, has made us His own special people. So if no one on this earth thinks you are special, God does and it is His opinion of us that matters.

The Bible is filled with scriptures telling us who we are and what

God has done for us because He loves us! So grab your Bible on a daily basis and search the scriptures!

Leah got over her challenges and at the end was able to praise her Lord! I got over my issues and 'what me has done to me' because if I didn't, I would have missed the gift that God had for me in the person of my husband, Bruce Mack!

So whatever you are facing, know that you can get over it because God has made you more than a conqueror, the Greater One lives on the inside of you.

What Me Has Done to Me

What a strange question to ask oneself
Something to think about indeed,
Because as I ponder on this thought
I'm aware that I'm in need.

For I have eaten unnecessarily
I have received junk into my heart,
I have carried other people's burdens
That weren't meant for me from the start.

I have held on to depression
And low self esteem for too long,
I must learn how to love myself
Breathe in God's Word to make me strong.

Negativity must get under
There's no place for you in me,
A brand new day is now approaching
A day of liberation I can see.

CHAPTER SIX

OVERCOMING THE PAIN WITHIN

"*...for we are well able to overcome it*" (Numbers 13:30)

What Pain? Who told you I was in pain? I am talking about the pain that you have experienced from being rejected. Whether you received the rejection from a parent, a family member or a lover, pain is within you because rejection and pain go hand in hand.

Sometimes we go to a place of denial and pretend that it does not or did not hurt. It is like the story tale of the Emperor's new clothes.

In this tale, by Hans Christian Anderson, an Emperor who cares for nothing but his wardrobe hires two weavers who promise him the finest suit of clothes from a fabric invisible to anyone who is unfit for his position or "just hopelessly stupid". The Emperor cannot see the cloth himself, but pretends that he can for fear of appearing unfit for his position or stupid. His ministers do the same. When the swindlers report that the suit is finished, they pretend to dress him. The Emperor then marches in procession before his subjects. Of course none of his subjects say anything about him parading about in his birthday suit; they all pretend that he is well dressed. Everyone is in denial, with the exception of a child. As the parade passes by, this child in the crowd calls out that the Emperor is wearing nothing at all and the cry is taken up by others. The Emperor cringes, suspecting the assertion is true, but holds his composure and proudly continues the procession.

Scholars have noted that the phrase 'Emperor's new clothes' has become a standard metaphor for anything that speaks of pretension and collective denial.

The child in the crowd exposed what was going on. He was the only one who was not walking in denial. Sometimes we can go on for years not admitting that we are in pain, but the only one we are fooling is ourself. Some of us have become so comfortable with the pain that we wear it like clothes, instead of exposing it and bringing it to the light so that it can be dealt with. Walking in denial when we need to be like the child in the story and say, "The pain is here and Lord, I need to be released from it!"

Why do we go into denial about the pain when we know it is there and that it is real? Is it because we are embarrassed and do not want anyone to know that we were rejected by someone like him? Our girl friends say things like, "Girl, you can do better than that," or "You are better off without him," but these words only increase the pain you are feeling.

There are those who have been rejected so much that the pain that accompanied rejection has caused them to behave differently than the way they used to.

There was a time when they were open and friendly to everyone. They walked in love and they believed the best in others. But after being rejected they are no longer open to everyone, they now handle people with a long handled spoon and they consider people guilty until proven innocent. Why has this happened? Since the pain was never released it has influenced every aspect of their life and altered their behavior.

Some women have chosen to cover up the pain. They know that the pain is there, but they believe that if they ignore it long enough, it will have no effect on them. Statements like... "I can handle it" are repeated over and over in their minds. Even thinking about it this very moment makes you want to toss this book aside and go watch a Lifetime movie.

We cover up the pain by throwing ourselves into work, school, or church activities to stay busy. This is only a cloak, and it does not do anything for the pain. It just keeps us overworked, stressed and burnt out.

We must acknowledge it in order to receive the healing we need. Even though we acknowledge it, we are not to dwell on it. Pain should not control our lives.

We must not place our focal point on the rejection, but we must fix our minds on the fact that we can overcome.

What we feel inside from being rejected is severe emotional and mental distress and it can rob us of our peace if we allow it. Our Example is Jesus, in Hebrews 12. It tells us in verse 2 that Jesus, who is the author and finisher of our faith, endured the cross and despised the shame because His focus was on the joy that was to take place after it was all over. He endured the rejection because He did not focus on it. He focused on the reality that His purpose was to provide the way for us to have fellowship with Him because of His blood washing away our sins. He also focused on the fact that He was going back to the Father, taking

His rightful place on the throne at the Father's right hand. He could have focused on how He went to His own people and they rejected Him. That had to cause Him pain. He loved them so much that we see Him weep. But He did not focus on that, He focused on "the joy". What are we focusing on? Have we decided to get free from this pain of rejection so that we focus on "the joy" that is meant for us?

We must forgive the person who rejected us, regardless of who it was and when it was, so that we can overcome it.

Once again our perfect example is Jesus He said while on the cross, "Father, forgive them for they know not what they do." Even though they did not know what they were doing by crucifying the Messiah, whom they waited for, they read about and heard prophecies concerning; Jesus knew. He knew because this was prophesied before the beginning of time that He was going to be the Ultimate Sacrifice and yet he could forgive them.

What about us? Sometimes when people hurt us, they do it on purpose. Are we supposed to forgive them in these cases too? My answer is yes. We are to forgive others if we want the Father to forgive us.

You may be saying to yourself, how can I forgive my mother who told me in front of the entire family that she did not want anything to do with me? How? You just do not know how much pain I felt when she said those words to me. I may not know, but Jesus knows and He says that you can forgive her and that He can fill that pain with His love. Then in turn you can begin to love her again. Even if she does not want to see you, you can still love her in your heart and God can fill that void. Remember that He is a miracle working God and that nothing is too hard for Him. He can repair that relationship, but you must do your part first and forgive her. Even if she never asks you to, you must do this for you. You must go to your Heavenly Father and ask Him for the strength to forgive her. He will honor that prayer and before you know it, when you think of her, it will not hurt any more. You can and will overcome this pain!

What about the marriage that you poured your heart and soul into and now your husband has decided he no longer wants to be married? Do you have to forgive him too? Yes, my dear sister, you must forgive him too in order for you to receive the healing you need to go on with your life. A number of things can happen if you choose not to forgive him.

You can become bitter and cold inside. Unforgiveness can eat at you like worms inside your body. It can eat at your love, your sweetness even your joy, just to name a few.

If you do not forgive him, you will begin to see all men as you see him. All men are not the same. With this attitude you will never receive the mate that God intends for you to have. You will push him away and refuse his love because you think that he will treat you like the other one did.

As long as you carry the pain inside and not forgive this man, you could re-marry and take your hurt out on this new husband and end up in another divorce. You must forgive so that God can heal you. You can overcome your pain so that you can move forward!

While we are this subject of forgiveness it is also important that you forgive yourself! Sometimes you can beat yourself up because of what you may have allowed yourself to get into, even after God has warned you. You find yourself in a relationship that was not His will. The relationship ends and you are in pain because of rejection. You then walk around in guilt and condemnation when you need to let it go. None of us are perfect. We all make mistakes. We are to learn from them and move on. Romans 8:1-2 tells us that there is no condemnation to those who are in Christ Jesus who walk not after the flesh, but after the Spirit. So if you have repented, God has forgiven you and you need to forgive yourself and move on in your faith.

When I blew it by not heeding the warning God gave me, I walked around in condemnation for so many years. Finally, someone told me I had to stop it, forgive myself and go on with my life. As long as I was holding on to unforgiveness I was going around in a circle. And when you go around in a circle you do not make any advancement anywhere. You see, hear and experience the same things over and over again. I was beating myself up and it was not doing me any good. So I had to forgive myself so that I could move forward in God.

Another thing about unforgiveness is that it blocks your growth. Remember I said it is like a worm that eats at you on the inside? Well it also keeps you from growing spiritually. It puts a halt on your growth, almost like a rubber band that binds you. It cuts off your circulation. In order for us to grow, we must be connected to the true vine. The true vine is Jesus Christ and that is where we get our growth from. Having a real relationship with the Word of God, Jesus, who according to John chapter 1 is the living Word of God. When a person has unforgiveness in their heart, they cannot stay connected to the vine because unforgiveness brings a separation. The vine is our source and He nourishes us with all we need. We need forgiveness to grow. If we do not forgive He cannot forgive us and that stops nourishment. Therefore, if we are not receiving our nourishment from the true vine, then unforgiveness will nourish us with anger, hatred, and resentment which will in turn build a fortress inside.

When a person's spiritual growth has been stunted, they are at a standstill. In some cases the person has completely left the will of God, unaware that they can overcome any pain.

The Bible says in Romans 8 verse 37 that we are more than conquerors which makes us overcomers. But in order to be an overcomer, we must overcome something; meaning we must 'come over' whatever it is. We must
win or be successful in spite of the obstacles. We must come over the pain that we have inside of us. We must release it to God and allow the healing to transform our lives.
You must 'come over' the pain your husband caused you when he no longer wanted to be married. You must 'come over' the pain your mother caused when she said she did not want to see you again. You must 'come over' the pain you experienced when you did not get the job promotion that should have been yours. You must 'come over' the friendship that ended abruptly and left your head spinning. You must 'come over' all of the rejection that you experienced in your life so that you can fulfill the purpose that God has for you.

Numbers 13:30 states, *"And Caleb stilled the people before Moses, and said, Let us go up at once, and possess it; for we are well able to overcome it."* In this passage of scripture, twelve spies had been sent to view the Promised Land that the Lord God had given the children of Israel. When the spies were in the land they saw that it was a good land filled with milk and honey, but they also saw giants in the land. So when they came back to give the report about the land, ten of the spies went on and on about the land being good, but there were giants in the land and the giants were so huge that they looked like grasshoppers in comparison. By this negative report they made all of Israel murmur and complain against Moses. They were preparing to stone him because they blamed him for leading them out of Egypt and into the hands of the giants.

Joshua and Caleb came back with a good report letting the people know that they were well able to overcome whoever was occupying their land. So they were doing all they could to get the people to trust and believe God. For after all, God had promised this land to them and since He was with them, they could handle the giants. This teaches us that whatever issue we may be facing, we are well able to overcome it! They had to deal with giants in the natural and the men of faith said, "We are well able to overcome it." We may be dealing with pain inside that is like a giant. This pain can be weighing us down, overlooking us, making us feel smaller in comparison, following us everywhere we go, but like Caleb said, we are well able to overcome it! The Greater one lives within us. He is Jesus Christ!

Even though there were giants in the land, the land still belonged to the children of Israel. This lets us know that sometimes it is not easy to get over the pain and rejection. Sometimes there is a fight ahead and we must go to war. We have spiritual weapons that are mighty through God and they are able to pull down strongholds or whatever it is that is holding us captive. Our weapons of prayer and praise are mighty and they can and do defeat the enemy; even the enemies of pain and rejection. We have what we need inside of us to defeat the enemy and overcome the rejection that has been holding on to our lives longer than it should have.

Notice that the giants were in possession of the land flowing with milk and honey which was Israel's Promised Land. What are the giants of pain and rejection keeping you from? Are they keeping you from walking in joy? Are they keeping you from walking in love and peace? Are they keeping you from your Promised Land?

Your Promised Land is a place of healing. You do not have to live with pain. This is not the will of God for your life. How do I know this? Jesus came to heal the broken hearted. The broken hearted are those whose feelings have been crushed by the husband who has gone off to be with another woman. The broken hearted are those whose feeling have been completely shattered because of giving out love and not receiving love in return from friends and family. The broken hearted are those who feel as though their heart has been broken into a million pieces because of the pain they are experiencing from being misused and abused.

Jesus knew that someone was going to break your heart and so He came. He knew that someone was going to make you feel worthless when they decided they no longer wanted to be with you and so He came. He knew that someone was going to say words to you that were going to hurt you all the way to your bones and so He came. He knew that the rejection you were going to face was going to cause you great pain and so He came. He is here for you; He is here to let you know that you are well able to overcome it!
You can get free right now, wherever you are, you can overcome your pain. Just repeat these words…

Heavenly Father, I come to you now in the name of your Son Jesus Christ. I acknowledge the fact that I have had this pain from rejection and I want to be free. I am tired of walking in denial. I am tired of covering up the pain with work, school, church and busyness. I forgive _____
(you fill in the blank) for rejecting me and hurting me. I ask you,

Father, to help me to forgive them because it is hard. I do not want to forgive them with just my mouth. I want to forgive them from my heart. I know that if I do not forgive them, you will not forgive me. I ask for your healing love to fill all voids in my heart and deliver me from all unforgiveness, anger, resentment and bitterness that has a hold of my life as well. Thank you for freeing me, for loving me and for blessing me right now. I give you praise! Amen.

Oh – the Pain

The pain that hurts like many arrows
Piercing through this heart of mine,
Even though you went on with your life
I was stuck like a leaf on a vine.

I was twisted inside all in knots
There were days when I just couldn't eat,
And yet, the Lord was there right beside me
Saying forgiveness must be your daily meat.

So I had to release those who had rejected me
Not just one, but I had to release them all,
In order for me to receive my healing
In order for me to answer His call.

You see I've been called to love my neighbor
To be an example of the love of the Lord,
I cannot do this with bitterness inside me
But I can with the Word which is my sword.

CHAPTER SEVEN

FROM PAIN TO PRAISE

"...and she said, Now will I praise the Lord: therefore she called his name Judah and left bearing." (Genesis 29:35)

I am sure by now that you are already rejoicing in what the Lord has done for you. For you have found out that the Lord hears you, He is joined to you, and you have overcome your pain! Glory to the Most High God! This chapter continues the story of Leah and concludes with her fourth son.

Have you ever been so heavy with despair, so messed up with the affairs of life that you were unable to give God praise? You may have gone through the motions, but inside your heart you knew that it just was not there; it was only lip service and your heart was far from God. Have you been there before and even got the t-shirt?

I believe this is how Leah felt. Sure, she acknowledged God throughout her years of bearing her sons, but she could not give God the praise in the midst of her rejection. She had to come through the affliction, the hatred and the separation before she could praise God.

Remember from Chapter One the scriptures let us know that **when** the Lord **saw** that Leah was hated, He **opened** her **womb.** From this we see that Leah did not focus on the fact that she was fruitful and multiplying, she only wanted to be loved. She did not even think about her sister who was barren, which was considered a curse at that time; she just wanted her husband to love her and be joined to her. During her childbearing years; she was birthing out the tribes of Israel, through pain, affliction, suffering, rejection and hatred. This lets us know that God has birthed gifts and callings inside of us that we must deliver. Sometimes they are birthed through hardships, trials and tribulations. We must bring them forth because God has put them inside of us for purpose. He chose us to do something that only we can do.

Think about the birthing process. When labor begins the mother is in serious pain, the baby is coming and the birthing canal is opening. This is all part of bringing forth the beautiful baby. When we are birthing things in the spirit, it comes forth as we labor. We experience contractions, and sometimes we want to abort, but the Holy Spirit is on the inside saying, "push." So we pray until something happens. We persevere until something happens. We refuse to give up because the baby, the gifts and callings are for the body of Christ to edify them. When the birth is complete, it is precious in the sight of the Lord.

It took Leah some time but she finally got it together. It is not easy having children, but to have them while your heart is hurting makes the pain even worse. Leah had a change of heart. She had now learned to put her focus on her Creator and her Lord. After she had gone through all of the drama in her life, something finally clicked. She had been through enough heartache and now instead of wallowing any longer, she decided to give God praise. What did she have to lose? Not one thing. I believe in my heart that once Leah praised God, she felt better. I know when I give God praise, I feel better. There is just something about praising the Awesome God that we serve!

She named her son Judah, which means praise. So every time she was calling her son's name she was saying "praise" and things were changing for her. They may not have been changing for her on the outside, but inside there was a change. You cannot praise God and dwell on your circumstances at the same time. You can only do one or the other. So whatever was taking place before she called Judah's name, once she said Judah or praise, things changed!

Praise changes the atmosphere. Making a joyful noise unto the Lord is good for the soul. Clapping your hands and lifting up the name of Jesus is a powerful instrument. There is so much power in praise that it even confuses the enemy. Allow me to give you an example of this found in II Chronicles 20: 14 – 24 (Amplified Bible)

> *"Then the Spirit of the Lord came upon Jahaziel son of Zechariah, the son of Benaiah, the son of Jeiel, the son of Mattaniah, a Levite of the sons of Asaph, in the midst of the assembly. He said, 'Hearken, all Judah, you inhabitants of Jerusalem, and you King Jehoshaphat. The Lord says this to you: Be not afraid or dismayed at this great multitude; for the battle is not yours, but God's. Tomorrow go down to them. Behold, they will come up by the Ascent of Ziz, and you will find them at the end of the ravine before the Wilderness of Jeruel. You shall not need to fight in this battle; take your positions, stand still, and see the deliverance of the Lord [Who is] with you, O Judah and Jerusalem. Fear not nor be*

dismayed. Tomorrow go out against them, for the Lord is with you.' And Jehoshaphat bowed his head with his face to the ground, and all Judah and the inhabitants of Jerusalem fell down before the Lord, worshiping Him. And some Levites of the Kohathites and Korahites stood up to praise the Lord, the God of Israel, with a very loud voice. And they rose early in the morning and went out into the Wilderness of Tekoa; and as they went out, Jehoshaphat stood and said, 'Hear me, O Judah, and you inhabitants of Jerusalem! Believe in the Lord your God and you shall be established; believe and remain steadfast to His prophets and you shall prosper.' When he had consulted with the people, he appointed singers to sing to the Lord and praise Him in their holy [priestly] garments as they went out before the army, saying, 'Give thanks to the Lord, for His mercy and loving-kindness endure forever!' And when they began to sing and to praise, the Lord set ambushments against the men of Ammon, Moab, and Mount Seir who had come against Judah, and they were [self-] slaughtered; For [suspecting betrayal] the men of Ammon and Moab rose against those of Mount Seir, utterly destroying them. And when they had made an end of the men of Seir, they all helped to destroy one another. And when Judah came to the watchtower of the wilderness, they looked at the multitude, and behold, they were dead bodies fallen to the earth, and none had escaped!"

In this portion of scripture, we see that the enemies of King Jehoshaphat, who was the King of Judah (praise), came against him to battle. King Jehoshaphat and his army were greatly outnumbered. He was afraid and began to seek the Lord as to what to do in this situation. God answered him and gave him the strategy. He told him that he was not going to have to fight this battle, but he was to let Judah go before them, meaning praise. This battle was fought with the singers and the praisers. The scriptures do not tell us if the armies heard the praise or not, but if they did, they probably had to be confused. They were to fight and not to hear a choir singing and praising. All the scripture tells us is that ambushes were set up by God. Israel's enemies were so confused that they killed each other. After it was over, the people of God collected the spoils from the enemy. If you could just realize how important and powerful it is to praise God in the midst of it all, you would not be walking around in despair.

Praise also brings deliverance. There is a story in Acts that talk about Apostle Paul and Silas, who were followers of Jesus. They had been thrown in prison for casting the devil out of a damsel. But at midnight while they prayed and sang praises the prison doors were opened. A man and his family were saved (delivered from their sins). (The story is found in Acts 16; read it when you get the chance and you will be blessed). Paul and Silas could have moaned and groaned about what was done to them, but instead they prayed and sang praises unto God. They knew that praise made all the difference in the world. They knew who they were, children of God, and they counted it a privilege to suffer for Christ. When the prison doors were opened, they could have walked out, but instead they stayed and ministered to the jailor. Praise is such a powerful tool.

After Leah had Judah, she left child bearing for a season. She had learned some valuable lessons. Even in birthing, there were lessons to be learned.

Think about this for a moment… Leah just wanted Jacob to love her and be joined to her. This was a reasonable request after all she was married to him. God heard and saw her. He knew what she was experiencing. He even felt her pain and He blessed her beyond what she could even ask or think. Leah did not know, but God knew that He was setting her up to be blessed. She just had to endure the heartache, the rejection and the pain. Because of her enduring she had another son, Judah.

I want to share this portion of scripture with you regarding Judah that is found

in the book of Genesis 49:8 – 10 (Amplified Bible)

> *"Judah, you are the one whom your brothers shall praise; your hand shall be on the neck of your enemies; your father's sons shall bow down to you. Judah, a lion's cub! With the prey, my son, you have gone high up [the mountain]. He stooped down, he crouched like a lion, and like a lioness--who dares provoke and rouse him? The scepter or leadership shall not depart from Judah, nor the ruler's staff from between his feet, until Shiloh [the Messiah, the Peaceful One] comes to Whom it belongs, and to Him shall be the obedience of the people."*

This is what was pronounced over Judah by his father Jacob. His brothers were going to bow down to him which was an awesome thing. What Leah received from suffering all those years, was a son that became the royal lineage. And out of this lineage not only came King David, but King Jesus!

Of course she was not alive to see this, but we see it and it is an example for us to see that out of pain comes praise!

Leah was so stuck on wanting love from a natural man that it kept her from praise. Once she got beyond that, she was praising God on a daily basis.

My precious sisters, if you are not being loved by the man of your dreams at this time do not waste this time. The word of God gives a beautiful word for the single women. In the book of I Corinthians 7:34 it states: *"The unmarried woman cares for the things of the Lord that she may be holy both in body and in spirit."* The unmarried woman seeks to please her Lord and she does this by being holy in body and in spirit. My advice for my single sister is to enjoy your singleness with just you and your Heavenly Father.

I believe that the unmarried Christians are the ones that the married Christians are sometimes jealous of. The reason I say this is because the unmarried has all the time in the world to care for the things of the Lord. They get to talk to their Father without interruption; they can work for him without having to ask someone's permission. If they choose to spend an entire Saturday in prayer and seeking the face of God, they can. When the unmarried leave their workplace at the end of the day, they can go home and relax in the presence of the Lord. It is just them and God and that is a wonderful thing!

Do not wait until you are joined with another to give God praise. God always deserves to be praised and we were created to give Him praise. We should not let anything stop us from giving

God the praise. We have so many reasons to praise him! The psalmist says in Psalm 34:1, *"I will bless the Lord at all times and His praise shall continually be in my mouth."* This should be a reality in every believer's life. Not just when things are going good, but even when things are not going your way or the way that you think they should. We are to give God thanks in every situation.

David was the one who wrote this Psalm. He was on the run from Saul and pretending to be insane so that a king named Achish would not kill him. With all of this going on in his life he was still able to give God praise.

So what is keeping you from praising your God? Is your heart hurting because of your baby's daddy? Did you give him all of your heart and he trampled on it? Are you hurting because you thought that he was going to be joined to you because you were carrying his child? Do you think that God does not love you because you messed up? Let me tell you something - in this Christian life, nothing is wasted; not our mistakes, not our failures, not our setbacks, nothing! God has said that He will cause <u>all</u> things to work together for our good because we love Him and we are the called according to His purpose. God is a forgiving God; all you have to do is repent. He is a loving God and will love you like no other will or can.

Let me encourage you and let you know, if you do not already... God has a purpose for your life. *"For I know the thoughts that I think toward you, saith the Lord, thoughts of peace, and not evil, to give you an expected end."* (Jeremiah 29:11). The thoughts that the Lord has of us, are not evil but of peace. The things that we go through at times rob us of our peace and keep us from praising God. If we would focus on this scripture, knowing that everything will be alright, we can give God praise.

God has a purpose for your life. You may not know what it is right now, but if you seek Him, He will reveal it to you. You were not put on this earth to walk around being depressed, hurt or rejected. God has never rejected you and He will not reject you. He has His arms open wide for you and He wants to demonstrate His love to you. Once you experience His love, nothing with compare. His love is holy, His love is pure, and His love does not stop because you may have gained some weight or you may not be a Miss America. God's love is so deep that it sweeps you right off of your feet.

So whatever you are going through right now, I want you to focus on your Heavenly Father. If you do not know Him, ask Him to come into your heart. Go to God the Father in prayer. Admit that you are a sinner and that you need a Savior. Believe that Jesus died on the cross for your sins and that He came to be your Savior. Believe that He rose again on the third day and is now in Heaven praying for you. Confess your sins to God. If you prayed and believe you are now a born again believer, glory to God!! Call someone you know that is a Christian and tell them you gave your heart to the Lord and begin praising Him! You just made the greatest decision that you will ever make in life, which is to become born again. Your life will never be the same! It will not be a bed of ease, but you will be able to handle it with Jesus living inside of you!

You need to get connected to a Bible believing church body where the Word of God is taught so that you can grow. Begin reading the Bible so that you can learn about this great God that you are now joined to.

Let me give you some reasons to praise God…

He woke you up this morning! He let you see a brand new day! He brought you out of darkness into His marvelous light! You have your health! You have your strength! He gave you brand new mercy! He is Faithful! He is your Healer! He is a forgiving God! He loves you with an everlasting love! He is your Savior! He is your Redeemer! He is your Deliverer! He is your Strong Tower! He is your Way Maker! He is your Covenant Keeper! He is your Friend that sticks closer than a brother! He is your Day! He is your Night! He is your Peace! He is your Light! He is your Help! He is whatever you need Him to be! He will never leave you nor forsake you! He is with you everywhere you go! He loves you like no one else can or does!

Do not wait a second longer. Wherever you are, put this book down, and give your God some praise!!

From Pain to Praise

I did not think I could get there
No longer carrying this pain,
Walking around with rejection
With tears coming down like the rain

I thought that this would always be with me
Like it was my destiny in this life,
I did not know it was not mine to bear
Inside me there was brokenness and strife

But I have now learned to Praise God
In the good times and in the bad,
Because He has been with me always
Even in those times when I am sad

That is why I have to praise Him
Because it does not hurt anymore,
He has birthed new joy inside me
For it is Christ whom I adore!

CHAPTER EIGHT

NO LONGER IDENTIFIED BY REJECTION

"And he, casting away his garment, rose, and came to Jesus."
(Mark 10:50)

Now that you have overcome your pain you should no longer be indentified by rejection. You may be saying to yourself, "Lauri, what on earth does that mean"? I am glad that you have asked that question.

A certain behavior that a person makes causes us to label that person and sometimes even judge them. For example if a woman gets angry at you when you bring up her past boyfriend who abused her, we would say that she is still identified with rejection. She has not released the pain and she is still in need of healing.

Before we go any further, let me tell you what the definition is of the word identified. It means to cause to be or become identical; to conceive as united (as in spirit, or principle); to be or become the same. So what Webster's dictionary is telling us is that if I identify myself with rejection, I have become united in spirit with that ugly spirit known as rejection. By looking at my life, how I act, the type of men I attract, all of this points to the fact that I have this spirit attached to me. I have become one with rejection.

How do you know that you have identified yourself with rejection? One way to know is if you put yourself down so that no one has the opportunity to do so. Have you ever been around a person who was always talking bad about themselves? This person is suffering with this spirit. They feel that no one wants to be bothered with them and no one thinks highly of them. They put themselves down because they do not want to be rejected or hurt by the words that someone else may say to them.

Another way to know if you are identified with rejection is you remove yourself from relationships and/or circumstances thinking that they will end up like all of the others. You do not even give them a chance. God could have sent you your life long partner, but you are still connected with rejection and so you sent him away. You are walking around in fear of being hurt and have not allowed the Holy Spirit to heal you so you can receive the promise He has for your life, your mate.

Remember you were freed in the last chapter and now you must act like it and walk in your deliverance. I know that it may not be easy and you may not be able to do it today, but soon you will. Remember: this Christian life is a faith walk and sometimes we must walk and then the manifestation comes.

I want to share two Bible characters that will help you in your identity change.

The first one is found in the book of Mark chapter 10 verses 46 – 52…

> *"And they came to Jericho: and as He went out*
> *of Jericho with His disciples and a great number*

*of people, blind Bartimaeus, the son of Timaeus,
sat by the highway side begging. And when he
heard that it was Jesus of Nazareth, he began
to cry out, and say, Jesus, thou son of David,
have mercy on me. And many charged him that
he should hold his peace: but he cried the more
a great deal, Thou son of David, have mercy on
me. And Jesus stood still, and commanded him
to be called. And they call the blind man, saying
unto him, Be of good comfort, rise; He calleth
thee. And he, casting away his garment, rose,
and came to Jesus. And Jesus answered and said
unto him, What wilt thou that I should do unto
thee? The blind man said unto him, Lord, that I
might receive my sight. And Jesus said unto him,
Go thy way; thy faith hath made thee whole. And
immediately he received his sight, and followed
Jesus in the way."*

In this passage of scripture, Jesus and His disciples were just
leaving Jericho. They had a crowd of people accompanying
them because Jesus was healing the sick, working miracles and
teaching the good news of the kingdom of heaven. There was this
blind man at the highway begging, which is what blind people
did during that time. They did not have public assistance as we
know it, therefore they did not have social security disability and
they were depending on the kindness of the people's hearts to
give to them so they could survive. Blind Bartimaeus heard that
Jesus was passing by. He was tired of living in his condition;
blind, begging, depending on people to survive. This is a key
point; you must get to the point that you are tired of living in
rejection and the spirits that accompany it in order to be freed
from it.

Back to our story, Bartimaeus knew that Jesus, the Son of David could heal him so he cried after Jesus to get his healing. The people were trying their best to quiet him down, but he cried all the more. What is hindering you from getting your identity change? I want to encourage you and say, "Do not let anything stop you from your change. Do not let negative thoughts, words of discouragement, the enemy, nothing. Keep pressing forward, onward and upward." Bartimaeus did not let the people stop him from calling out to Jesus. He did not give up. Giving up is one of the friends of rejection. Bartimaeus could have said, "Forget it, these people are in my way, they know that I cannot see and they are just being selfish wanting Jesus to themselves." He could have said, "Maybe next time He comes around I will get the chance to speak to Him. There are too many people today." He did not say any of these things because he was sick of being in the situation he was in and he was not going to let this opportunity pass him by. He knew that Jesus was the Son of David because he knew that the Messiah would be a descendant from David and therefore he believed He was the one and He was able to heal him. I pray that you are grasping what I am telling you so that you can walk in your identity change. Do you believe that Jesus is who He says He is? Do you believe that He came to mend the broken hearted and to set them who are captive free? If you no longer want to be identified with rejection, you must believe this without a shadow of a doubt.

Once Jesus heard Bartimaeus through the crowd, he called for him. It is very important to pay close attention to what Bartimaeus did before he went to Jesus. The Bible states that he cast away his garment, in other words he took off his coat. The coat that the blind beggars wore identifying them with blindness, he removed it even before he went to Jesus. Notice that he removed the coat before he even stood up. So, before he moved from his position naturally, he took the coat off as an act of faith. He was telling those around him that as of that particular point in time, he was no longer united with blindness because as far as he was concerned he was already healed. Once Jesus called him, it was a done deal. He was walking by faith and not by sight, which is what you need to do.

If you have overcome your pain and have forgiven the person or people who have hurt you and rejected you, you must now walk like it. You may have just prayed this prayer a little while ago, but it is now time to walk it out. Just like Bartimaeus before you get up, before you change positions you must cast off the coat of rejection. You may have to just declare it to yourself and say, "I am no longer identified with rejection. I am no longer one with that spirit, I have been set free and I am walking in my liberty, for who the Son makes free is free indeed!"

The other Bible character that I want to tell you about is Jacob, who is actually Leah's husband. He had an identity change and it is found in the book of Genesis 32:24 – 29

> *"And Jacob was left alone; and there wrestled a man with him until the breaking of the day. And when he saw that he prevailed not against him, he touched the hollow of his thigh; and the hollow of Jacob's thigh was out of joint, as he wrestled with him. And he said, 'Let me go, for the day breaketh.' And he said I will not let thee go, except thou bless me. And he said unto him, 'What is thy name'? And he said, Jacob. And he said, 'Thy name shall be called no more Jacob, but Israel: for as a prince hast thou power with God and with men, and hast prevailed.' And Jacob asked him, and said; tell me, I pray thee, thy name. And he said, 'Wherefore is it that thou dost ask after my name'? And he blessed him there."*

In this portion of scripture, Jacob was left alone. He was all alone because he sent his wives and maidservants and children away for their safety. Genesis chapters 25 and 27 tell the story of how Jacob deceived his father Isaac and somehow bought the birthright from his brother Esau. The birthright was given to the oldest and with it came blessings and benefits that those after the first born were not entitled to. Well, when Jacob tricked his father and received the blessings of the birthright, Esau was furious and purposed in his heart to kill him. Jacob had to leave town. He went to live with his uncle Laban for a number of years and it was now time for him to go back to his own land, according to the Word of the Lord. When Jacob heard that Esau was on his way to meet him with 400 men, he was terrified and sent his loved ones away so they would not be killed.

Now, here we have Jacob all alone wrestling with a man all night long. Most scholars believe that this was an angel not an ordinary man. He wrestled so with this angel that the angel had to put his thigh out of joint. Jacob was determined not to let him go until he blessed him. This reminds me of Blind Bartimaeus. He was not going to let the opportunity to receive his sight pass him by. Whoever Jacob believed this angel was, he was not going to let him go until he received a blessing. He needed help; he did not want his family to die. He was tired of living according to his birth name which was Jacob which means supplanter from the word supplants. This word means to take the place or position of somebody by force or deception which is what Jacob did to get the birthright. Once he went home he no longer wanted to be identified with being a deceiver, he needed an identity change. God changed his name to Israel which means to struggle, to wrestle, to contend and prince of God. Instead of people calling him "Deceiver," they were calling him "Prince of God"

By the changing of his name, this changed his entire nature. When he finally met his brother Esau, Esau was no longer angry and they just loved on each other. He was no longer identified with being a deceiver, but a prince, just by changing his name made a difference in his life!

So what is it you must do so that people no longer identify you with rejection? I do not think that you have to change your name or your garment naturally, but you have to take some type of action so that everyone knows that rejection is no longer a part of your life.

When I think of a blind person, a white cane with a red tip and dark sunglasses come to mind. Just as we can recognize a blind person by these items, we can recognize you if you are still holding on to those things that say, "Look at me, I am suffering with rejection."

When I was bound by the spirit of rejection, I walked around in self pity and felt that no one wanted me. I did not care how I looked so I ate whatever was in sight. I did not care what I wore and so whatever fit, I put on; my thought was it did not matter because no one wanted me anyway. When you have this spirit as a part of your life, you are in gloom and despair. Like a line from a song that was sung on the TV Show Hee Haw, "gloom despair and agony on me" (written by Buck Owens and Roy Clark). That is how I felt and I had Christ in my life, but I was in the grip of this spirit and it had me in its clutches.

Now that I am free, no longer can anyone look at me and see that I am walking around bound by the spirit of rejection because I am not. My outlook has changed. I started being more conscience of what I was eating and what I chose to wear. I started buying clothes that were pretty and received compliments about my new way of dressing. I started loving me. It did not matter that I did not have a natural man in my life, because I had the Man, Christ Jesus in my life and He made me feel great!

Just as Jacob did not let the angel go until he blessed him, you have to be just as persistent with God to change you so that you are no longer identified with rejection. You may have to wrestle all night, but whatever you have to do, do it, you will love the change.

You may have to change the company you keep. I am sure that you have heard the saying, "birds of a feather flock together." I have learned that people suffering with rejection hang around other people who are suffering with rejection as well. They sit around and tell each other their stories of rejection and neither one are the better, because it feeds that spirit and causes it to become even stronger.

Once you are free, the devil does not want you to remain free, so you must walk in your liberty. You must declare that you are free. When someone wants to bring up your past, you stop them in their tracks and tell them you are free and you have no intentions of reverting back to your old ways. You have forgiven the person or people who hurt you and now you can walk with your head high, looking good and feeling fine. You know that we walk by faith and not by sight. As you continue to walk and read the Word of God, you will become more and more free because the Word of God delivers us. Even if it still hurts you, continue to walk and the pain will go away. There will come a time when you can look at that person, or those people in the face and declare that you love them. It may not be today, it may not be tomorrow, but it will come as you continue the faith walk.

So now you must ask yourself this question, "Now that I am no longer identified with rejection, what do I want to be identified with"? I am sure that if you are a born again believer, you want to be identified with Christ. When people see you, you want them to see Christ. Christ is love, joy and peace. You want to be recognized as someone who is filled with the joy of the Lord. Joy does not depend on outward circumstances, but it is based on an inward relationship with Jesus Christ.

When you were walking around suffering from rejection, you were walking around heavy and in despair, but now you have tossed that garment aside and you are wearing the garment of praise. This garment is light, and enjoyable.

You want to be identified with the word acceptance, which is the opposite of rejection. You have been accepted by the Beloved, you are His and He is yours. Jesus walks with you and you have conversation with Him and you are having such a spiritual love affair. It is heavenly!

You want to be identified as the sister who now has a ministry for hurting women. You have a testimony to tell, you have a story to share with those who are going through what you have been through. You can now tell them that you were hurt and you never thought the pain would ever go away. You can tell them that God has removed your pain and you can forgive and love. You can share with them that it was not easy, but you made it over and now with confidence you can declare that you are no longer depressed, lonely and sad. What a glorious word to give to someone. I am so thankful that Jesus is the same yesterday, today and forever. The healing power that He rose with on Calvary is still bringing healing today.

My precious sister, you have changed your garment, you have changed your name and now you can go onto the next level in your walk with the Lord.

You can boldly say that, "Rejection does not live here any longer!"

Rejected – not me

I did it - I changed my garment
Can't you see?
I am brand new
Rejected – not me.

I am walking by faith
And not by sight
The manifestation is coming
As I continue in the light.

No longer united with depression
Anger, rejection or sadness
I am done with hating, bitterness
And all of that madness.

A new creation in Christ
Can't you see?
I am brand new
Rejected – not me!